Sociologies of childhood an thinking

Berry Mayall

First published in 2003 by the Institute of Education, University of London
20 Bedford Way, London WC1H 0AL
www.ioe.ac.uk

Over 100 years of excellence in education

© Institute of Education, University of London 2003

Berry Mayall asserts the moral right to be identified as the author of this work.

All rights reserved. No part of this publication may be reproduced, stored in a retrieval system, or transmitted in any form or by any means, electronic, mechanical, photocopying, recording or otherwise, without the prior permission of the copyright owner.

British Library Cataloguing in Publication Data:
A catalogue record for this publication is available from the British Library

ISBN 0 85473 694 8

Design by Andrew Chapman
Typeset by Brigid Hamilton-Jones
Printed by Pear Tree Press Limited, Stevenage, Hertfordshire

Institute of Education • University of London

Sociologies of childhood and educational thinking

Berry Mayall

Professor of Childhood Studies

Based on an inaugural Professorial Lecture delivered at the Institute of Education, University of London on 15 October 2003

Acknowledgements

I am grateful to Priscilla Alderson, Virginia Morrow and Ann Oakley, who commented on an earlier version of this paper. Also to colleagues at the Social Science Research Unit for discussions over many years. And especially to hundreds of children, their mothers and teachers, who have provided me with opportunities to learn during the course of many research projects.

Sociologies of childhood and educational thinking

Introduction

I have worked at the Institute of Education for exactly 30 years this month. For almost a third of its illustrious history. I could start this talk with light-hearted reflections on how research has changed since the days when data analysis was by knitting needle.[1] I could also make some comments, as seems to be common on this kind of occasion, about my local hero. In my case this is Charles Dickens, who took a passionate interest in education, including Froebel. And who never wavered in his argument that decent housing, clean water and sanitation were prerequisites for progress in school.[2] A point still relevant today. But I want to press on with the substance of this talk. So my fascinating comments on these two topics are relegated to the notes to this paper.

This is a interesting year for rhetoric on education. It even seems possible that the great tanker of education practice is about to turn, fuelled by ideas about how children learn, about creativity, about participation; setting its course away from children as objects of the education system, and towards children as active learners, engaged, excited and joyful (DfES 2003b). I began to write this paper in March

2003, and have had to revise it several times, to take account of the latest pronouncements coming out of the DfES. I hope that some of what I have written will soon be out of date. But I think the general point – that we need good theories of childhood as bases for policy and practice – still holds.

While assembling ideas for this talk, I did some reading and attended several lectures on education topics. The emphasis tended to be on adults. Policy-makers, managers, teachers and parents. One evening I read an article in the *Guardian* (Tuesday 11 March 2003) about the recent described-as-astonishing achievements in Tower Hamlets, where GCSE and A level results have markedly improved. The article was about education service staff, councillors and teachers and about all the great things they had done. Nowhere in this account were the people at the centre of the education system, those who attend schools, who actually take these exams. Another way of looking at success in Tower Hamlets is through studying the young people themselves: the social contexts of their thinking, how they rate educational achievement; what they think school is for. As Katie Gavron (1997) did in her study of new generations of Bangladeshi young people in Bethnal Green and their motivations towards schooling and education.

It seems that children themselves have not been at the centre of educational thinking and of public debate on the education system. Or rather, perhaps, children are taken for granted, within traditional paradigms. Why is this? Essentially the answer is that adults are happy with their power over children and over childhood, and do not wish to face challenges to those powers inherent in serious analysis of the social status of childhood. The perceived function of schools – as socialisation for future citizens – is a powerful paradigm, inhibiting uncomfortable questions about the present tense of childhood. Another answer is that at university level most of the audience for education thinking, including the sociology of education, are teachers in training and managers – and they want to know about their own work and how to think about it (Reid 1978: 20, 26).

Children, as valued people living their lives now, tend not to be discussed in education thinking. This is true, too, in other areas of social life. Anthropologists have provided interesting discussion on how and why children and childhood itself have not been included in descriptions of how society works. The discussion centres on concepts of the person. In some definitions, a 'person' is someone who carries out socially significant activities. Needless to say – in some societies, only men are judged to do so. They do visible activities in the public world, valued by men. Women cannot reach personhood in such societies and children, also needless to say, are nowhere (La Fontaine 1998). Children are non-persons, since what they do is not identified and not valued. In our 'western' societies, it has taken feminist critiques of the presumed divide between the public and the private worlds to force recognition that women do socially useful things, even where their actions are hidden from public view. Children are next on the list. One of the last major social groups to be upgraded.

In the early to mid-nineteenth century in the UK, most children, as paid workers in the public domain, could be readily understood as socially useful – to their parents and to the economy more generally. But during the time when children were being taken out of household and paid work and put into schools, we also see the growth of the idea of children as non-contributing, as a cost to parents and the state, the child as in a preparatory stage of life. Hence, the child as socially use less, though emotionally precious (Zelizer 1985). The rise of child development studies neatly, and not at all by chance, chimed in with and reinforced such ideas. Ellen Key (1909) wrote a manifesto for a *Century of the Child* in 1900. But, in the twentieth century: 'Instead of a century of the child we got the century of the child professions' (Stafseng 1993: 77).

My topic today is the sociology of childhood. This paper is about the urgent importance of bringing into play new sociological approaches to childhood. These are needed to improve basic conceptual thinking about how society works. They are also needed as a matter of social justice. They are needed as theoretical bases for educational reforms. What are the key points in the sociology of childhood? How can the sociology of childhood help us in the current fashionable quest for ways of rethinking the education system?

We are concerned here with the social and political status of childhood. And with how we may complement the insights of psychological approaches with more sociological ones. And how such insights may help us think about the education system we have in this country. I go on now to make some points under three main headings:

- Traditional sociological thinking about childhood
- Recent developments in the sociology of childhood
- How the sociology of childhood can help educational thinking.

Berry Mayall

Traditional sociological thinking about childhood

Traditionally in the UK, children and childhood have had low status within mainstream sociology. Their low status has rested on the two complementary interlocking concepts: socialisation theory and child development theory (Jenks 1996: Chapter 1). Thus, under Parsonian functionalism, children have been understood as *socialisation* projects within the private domain. Like women in the 1950s, children are unproblematically assigned to the home. Durkheim has a lot to answer for here. In writing about education at the end of the nineteenth century, he sees women's work at home as simple, unthinking and 'homely'; essentially as preliminary to the more complex work undertaken at school. He described women's socialisation work on children thus:

> For it is the family that can distinctively and effectively evoke and organise those homely sentiments basic to morality and – even more generally – those germane to the simplest personal relationships.
>
> (Durkheim 1961: 19)

For 'family' read 'mother'. And note that within this model children are essentially passive. And that women's moral teaching rests not on cognitive strength, but on 'homely' uncontested, received tradition, whereby mothers will teach their children conformity with social norms. And, even more contentious: that mother–child relations are simple.

Feminists, of course, have challenged the notion that what they do at home is natural and simple, and that it is not to be defined as work. But few academics including feminists, of any kind, challenge received, traditional, sociological ideas about childhood.[3] Though mainstream sociology has moved on from functionalism to all sorts of isms (such as postmodernism, post-structuralism) mainstream sociologists have not included childhood in their re-thinking. Mainstream sociological thinking on childhood has remained obdurately functionalist. For instance, a trawl through recent introductory texts on sociology reveals that the authors do not recognise the existence of a sociology of childhood. Children are discussed, briefly, as adult-to-child socialisation projects within the family and education system, with some emphasis on the child as victim (Browne 1998; Fulcher and Scott 1999; Haralambos, Holborn and Heald 2000; Giddens 2001; Bilton *et al.* 2002).

I used to think it odd that sociologists, though keen to move from functionalism and espouse all manner of postmodernisms and post-structuralisms, have left children – conceptually – within functionalism, in a private, pre-social domain, objects of top-down socialisation. Perhaps this is because, whilst they love discussing new and ever more complicated isms, they are mainly interested in studying themselves – their own age-group.[4] More importantly: to understand childhood, as contributory to the workings of the social order, is to issue a challenge to power relations between adults and children. As Chris Jenks put it (1996: 21), there is an 'unreflexive gerontocentrism at the heart of socialisation theory'.

A striking instance of sociological blindness to childhood is within the sociology of the body. Now anyone who lives with children or has lived with children, knows that bodily relations are central to social relations between children and adults, yet in the sociology of the body (fashionable from the 1990s), children figure only briefly, as precursors to their adult status (e.g. Shilling 1993: Chapter 7; Turner 1992: 34, 40, 251). More recently, it has fallen to childhood sociologists to make some comments on this strange omission (Mayall 1998; Prout 1999).[5]

The second major plank in traditional sociological understandings of childhood is, of course, *developmentalism*. And here we have to draw distinctions between the complex, systematic and revelatory work carried out in academia, and the simpler – indeed cliché-ridden – understandings of those who make policy and practice. For brevity here I use the term 'the public mind' to include the understandings of those government ministers, civil servants, local authorities and so forth. Academic work on children's development has been marked by great thoroughness and subtlety, and it has moved towards highly interesting consideration of social dimensions in recent years (Cole 1996; Kagitcibasi 1996; Rogoff 1990). In this work the child as learner in social interaction has moved centre stage.[6]

But those important trends in psychological research and writing about children are not what the public mind focuses on. The public mind has latched on to one central belief: that the key thing about children is that they develop – they mature, they move from incompetence to competence, over time and during an organised, measurable journey (Jenks 1996: Chapter 1). The notion that children are best understood as incompetent vulnerable becomings who progress with adult help through stages needed to turn them into mature adults has socially recognised status; it is enshrined in policies and practices affecting children's lives. The public mind thinks of children in terms of their futures, and in terms of adult maturity and competence as the gold standard. The present tense of childhood matters much less.

But how childhood is lived, here and now, in the present, depends largely on social policies; and these in turn reflect understandings of childhood, and visions of child–adult relations. Of interest to us here are parochial understandings in the UK, and, in particular, New Labour's policies, especially as regards education. On taking power, New Labour enthusiastically accepted and developed Conservative policies on education. During its six years of government, traditional ideas about socialisation and development have fitted tightly with New Labour's specific concerns. Its concern has been with children as investment, children as capital for the future. New Labour has shown concern for child poverty, since poverty in childhood can throw long shadows forward and what matters is the adulthood of these children. But the principal theme has been socialisation, or training within a contained environment – the family, the school – towards citizenship, in the future. New Labour has not trusted children; they cannot be allowed to choose; rather they must be given clear direction (Hendrick 2003: 253). Perhaps New Labour politicians have also found endorsement for their traditional adult fear and suspicion of children, because they have read Ulrich Beck. Beck's thesis on individualisation in the 'risk society' provides a vision of young people making their own way, in their own way.[7] In the risk society, traditional boundaries and constraints have broken down, and people's life trajectories are not necessarily tied to those of their parents. So each individual young person:

must therefore learn, on pain of permanent disadvantage, to conceive of himself or herself as the centre of action, as the planning office with respect to his/her own biography, abilities, orientations, relationships and so on.

(Beck 1992: 135)

This must not be allowed to happen, New Labour has reasoned. Control, guidance, training, supervision are what is needed to restrain children and to channel them as required (for discussion see Prout 2000). And this vision allows little space for children's rights, which ultimately are about self-determination (Freeman 2000).

It is banal but also important to note that the clichéd version of developmental psychology has captured the attention of many UK policy-makers, as well as many of those who work with and for children: lawyers, social workers, teachers, doctors and nurses. The concerns and the paradigms of the late nineteenth century resonate today. The emergence of children into public view in state-sponsored schools provoked keen professional interest in the welfare, health, education and future productiveness of children (Rose 1985; Hurt 1979). The socialisation of children, towards their future usefulness, was complemented by psychological studies on children's development from immaturity to the gold standard of adult maturity.

But whilst that story may hold for the UK, it does not fit with the history of some other countries (Mackinnon 2003). In the Nordic countries, the child as agent and the child as citizen with rights have a long history. So we have to take into account the social histories of childhood within varying societies (Pringle 1998; Therborn 1993, 1996; Mayall 2002: Chapter 8). Until relatively recently, children in Nordic countries were workers in household economic enterprises; their value was recognised as economic as well as social. Furthermore, these countries came late to industrialisation, and to building up the prosperous states we now see. These factors may account for the high value put on children – on their contributions, now, as workers in school, as well as on their status as valued citizens, now and for the future (Therborn 1996; Gordon, Holland and Lahelma 2000). In addition, Nordic countries have relatively low variations in household income (compared to the UK); they have highly developed welfare states; and they also have small populations. The value of people is not judged according to their socio-economic position. Every child counts. By contrast in the UK, we have a society which industrialised and urbanised early, which took children out of the workplace early, which firmly established lower classes in opposition to higher classes, and which set in place an education system that both solidified and perpetuated social class differences and tensions. We have a society where high proportions of the population are denigrated and neglected. Some children are more highly valued than others. Instead of universalism, we have initiatives – including educational initiatives – targeted at the poor, and these, many people argue, perpetuate stigma and failure (Hendrick 2003: Chapter 6).

If we apply the UN Convention on the Rights of the Child to this comparison, using the 3Ps (protection, provision and participation) as guidelines, we can see differing emphases in the UK as compared to Nordic countries. Notably, it was England that pioneered the most massive abuse of children (during the early industrialisation period) and also then pioneered child-protection organisations (such as Barnardos, founded in 1866, the Children's Society founded in 1881[8] and the National Society for the Prevention of Cruelty to Children, founded in 1889); these played a considerable part in the development of protective legislation against child abuse. The Children Act 1908 provided a basic protective roof for children (Therborn 1993: 129; Hendrick 1994: Chapter 2). The emphasis on protection was taken up with renewed vigour in the 1980s and 1990s, when social services' work for children had to focus almost exclusively on child-abuse issues (Holman 2001: Chapter 5). Today in the UK adults still focus on protection as the guiding light for relations between the generations; they rally to the flag of protecting children and even, to some extent, of providing for children; whereas there is less popular support for children's participation.

Recent developments in the sociology of childhood

In the last twenty years or so, the sociology of childhood has developed fast. For discussion, I suggest that we may separate out – somewhat – three kinds of sociologies of childhood (Alanen 2001). Of course, these overlap and intersect; not least when one tries to link personal troubles to social and political issues. These three strands are: the sociology of children, the social construction of childhood, and structural sociologies of childhood.

It is relevant to start by noting that the sociology of childhood and the children's rights movement have drawn attention (broadly speaking) to two interwoven strands inherent in the definition of some people as children. And the concept of vulnerability runs through and across both. There is first the area of inherent vulnerability: physical weakness, lack of knowledge and experience, though these diminish rapidly as, from birth onwards, very small children engage with the social and physical world around them. It is these biological vulnerabilities that demand adult provision and protection. Secondly there is socially constructed vulnerability, the ideas, policies and practices that adults put into place which confirm children in social inferiority and dependence. Children are vulnerable because adults do not respect their rights; they lack political, social and economic power. A serious problem is that adults commonly collapse and confuse the two kinds of vulnerability, with the aim of naturalising childhood. Children may be perceived as developmentally incompetent, when it is social structures and social policies that deny them the opportunities to develop competence (Lansdown 1994: 34–5). The social position of women provides a clear analogy (Oakley 1994). The emphasis in the UN Convention on the Rights of the Child on protection, provision and participation rights arises from the perception that the interactions of biological and socially constructed vulnerabilities indicate the need for special efforts to respect those rights.

The sociology of children

The emphasis here is on children as social agents. In the sociology of children, children are agents in their learning, from their earliest days. Children do things that make a difference to relationships and to their own lives. Children have knowledge about what matters to them. They make assessments of events and of relations. They have clear moral sense, learned from their earliest encounters with dilemmas in daily life (Dunn 1988; Damon 1990).

These ideas are familiar – they make sense to psychologists and to people who live with children. Though possibly not to the 'public mind'. These ideas also have a long history in fiction, from Charles Dickens, through George Eliot, L.P. Hartley, D.H. Lawrence and the huge libraries of fiction written for children. Here for example – offered as literary refreshment – is Pip reflecting on his sister's harsh behaviour, when bringing him up 'by hand'.

> In the little world in which children have their existence, whosoever brings them up, there is nothing so finely perceived and so finely felt as injustice.... Within myself, I had sustained, from my babyhood, a perpetual conflict with injustice. I had known, from the time I could speak, that my sister, in her capricious and violent coercion, was unjust to me. I had cherished a profound conviction that her bringing me up by hand gave her no right to bring me up by jerks.
> (Charles Dickens, *Great Expectations*, [first published 1861–2] Chapter 8)

In terms of quantity of research, the sociology of children has been popular. It was the declared aim of the recent UK ESRC Children 5–16 Programme (1997–2000) that children as social actors should take central place in the funded projects. The widespread sympathy for this proposition may partly account for the huge numbers of applications to do these projects. Numbers of applications exceeded all previous records for ESRC Programmes. Of 307 applications, 22 – or 7 per cent – were funded. (Of these 22, four were based at the Institute – more than at any other institution. Well done the Institute!)[9]

The projects on the ESRC Programme and others funded, for instance, by the charitable foundations and trusts, are now providing a mass of detail, collected with children, on how children understand and experience a range of events and circumstances – ranging from ordinary daily life at home and school, to child abuse, migration and refugee status, illness and disability, and parental separation.[10]

This work within the sociology of children has been carried out around the world. Children are providing information about how they understand and value their working lives, their families, their education, their futures. Children have talked about living with violence and war (Johnson *et al.* 1998; Hart 1997). Child-to-Child, based first at the Institute of Child Health from 1979 and here at the Institute since 1987, has pioneered world-wide work which promotes children's participation in community development (Young and Durston 1987; Gibbs, Mann and Mathers 2002).

And of course a necessary part of the work of listening to children has been to consider good methods of doing so; there are now many books and papers on this; and they in turn help raise the status of children and of childhood because they point to children's competence as research participators and partners (Christensen and James 2000; Johnson, Hill and Ivan-Smith 1995).

One reason for the popularity of the sociology of children is researchers' empathy for the children's rights movement. This has worked in complement to and in collaboration with the sociology of children. There is two-way benefit. Children's rights to protection, provision and participation provide a structure for studying children's experiences. Children's experiences and what they reveal feed into the work of the children's rights movement, in its aim of describing the rights and wrongs of children's lives.

The social construction of childhood

Here the point is to draw attention to diversity across time and space in how childhood is defined and put into practice. This social constructionist approach draws on, for instance, an established body of work from historians, who point to changes over time; for instance in England, the Romantic child, the evangelical child, the factory child, the delinquent child, the schooled child, the psycho-medical child and the welfare child (Hendrick 1990, 2003; Cunningham 1991). Recent media attention to child abuse and to child crime has led critics to deconstruct the child as victim and the child as threat (Wyness 2000); and to consider how people's concepts of childhood itself are challenged by children who step out from comfortable paradigms, and, for instance, care for their disabled parents (Aldridge and Becker 2002), or kill other children (James and Jenks 1996).

Social constructionism draws attention to ways in which people's understandings of childhood relate to wider social and political issues (Prout and James 1990). We can see the child as defined (or 'constituted') in order to serve the purposes of certain adult versions of how society should operate. The rapid growth of developmental psychology – its acceptance as *the* way of thinking about children and childhood just at the time when children emerged into public prominence as state school pupils – is an example of the way concepts complement and underpin policy. People needed to re-formulate concepts about children and childhood at the time when they had to think about a state education system. Durkheim was positioned as sociologist and educationalist at a good time to propose and get accepted his version of the concept of socialisation – by adults – first at home and later at school.

In terms of action, these social constructs of childhood provide guidance for both adults and children. They tell adults how to organise childhoods, what childhood should consist of, how to decide whether a child is getting a good childhood. They also provide scripts for children – as in a play; they provide patterns or modes of living for children. In my own recent empirical work with a range of children, I found that some had very clearly articulated ideas about how childhood should be lived – among them Muslim children who quoted their parents' and teachers' prescriptions. Other children were living equally prescribed lives, but they less readily listed a set of principles and requirements handed down by parents (Mayall 2002: especially Chapter 4).

There are generational points here, too. At the socio-political level, we can see how childhoods are constructed to serve adult ends. At the more personal, interactive level, people who are parents now had childhoods that differed from the childhoods their children are living through. Present-day childhoods have been structured by a range of forces that make them very different from childhoods lived earlier in time. My own childhood in the 1940s differs from my daughter's childhood in the 1970s and from her children's childhoods now (see also Zeiher 2003 for a West German example). Nowadays traffic danger and stranger danger have forced children out of public places and spaces; the child as victim and the child as threat are commonplace understandings in the media. On the other hand, technologies are providing experiences unknown to older people (Hengst 2003; Buckingham 2000; Wyness 2000). So as children and their parents negotiate the character of childhoods now, both social groups have to deal with their differing experiences and understandings of childhood.

Structural sociology of childhood

The argument here is that childhood is a *permanent component of the social structure*, of the social order. It may be differently defined – or constructed – at differing times and places, but it is always there. Those people defined as children have always been subjected to the authority of adults; and so adults make special arrangements for childhood. Legal frameworks and conventions recognise children's distinctive social status. As I noted earlier, the UN Convention on the Rights of the Child was developed in recognition of the argument that children need adult protection and provision, and that their subordinate social position requires particular efforts to ensure respect for their participation rights. Institutions get set up specifically for children. For instance, Great Ormond Street Hospital was founded in the 1850s on the (then new) argument that children's illnesses were different from those of adults and needed special knowledge and care. Preventive health care services were established for UK children (and their mothers) long before such services for other social groups (Hurt 1979; Bruce 1979: 222–6). And, of course, schools, in most countries, are designed for children, rather than for citizens generally.

Sociology traditionally focused on work, as a major theme. Sociology became established in western societies during historical processes of industrialisation, in order to explain how the social order works; and in particular to explore the division of labour and its connections to the development of the market. Just as women have had to fight to make their contributions visible and respected, so efforts are underway on behalf of children. Over the last 20 years, *social usefulness* (the anthropological term) has been a major theme taken up by sociologists of childhood, in their attempts to show that children can be conceptualised as contributors, as inhabiting a social status that contributes to the maintenance and transformation of the social order. This way of thinking is proposed in macro-sociological analyses, by, notably, Jens Qvortrup (1985), who argues that children's social usefulness has shifted from their paid work to their learning work.

> Children take part in socially necessary activities, contribute towards the accumulation of knowledge and labour power to be used in society, are permanently a part of social renewal, and from an early age are an integral part of social organisation.
>
> (Qvortrup 1985: 142)

An important strand in recent sociological thought about children, then, is to understand them as carrying out socially useful, indeed necessary activities. We can extrapolate, and argue that these socially useful activities include learning, paid and unpaid work and people work (Stacey 1981: 186). Thus children can be properly understood as active agents in getting an education. In learning both at home and at school. As to paid work, varying estimates are that between two-thirds and three-quarters of UK children do some paid work before the school-leaving age of 16 (Mizen, Bolton and Pole 1999).[11] As to unpaid work: children carry out household maintenance; for instance in one study 30 per cent of boys and 50 per cent of girls described their jobs around the home (Morrow 1994: 132). They also participate in people work: in building, maintaining and promoting personal relations. These actions include looking after their parents; and maintaining relations with family members who live elsewhere, such as fathers and grandparents (Mayall 2002: Chapter 4). Children engage in friendships with other children, not only for the intrinsic value of these social relations, but as defence in the adult-ordered regime of school. Thus in the so-called public domain, and in the so-called private domain, I argue, children are contributors to the making and re-making of the social order.

That children do socially useful activities is a compelling argument. And this argument throws emphasis on the present tense of childhood. What they are doing now, is not preparation; it is active and interactive engagement with the social world around them. In pursuit of learning, they harness their knowledge, intelligence, their friends and their teachers. In pursuit of fun as well as learning, they interact with computers and the internet. In paid and unpaid work, they contribute to the economy of their households. In social relations, they play their part in making and sustaining relations, with their family members, and with other children.

Nevertheless children, at any rate in England, have low social status. (A reason for isolating England here is that commissioners for children have been established in Scotland, Wales and Northern Ireland, but not in England.) We can understand English children best as a minority social group. The topic for study then is how children as a minority social group inter-relate with the corresponding social group – adults. Childhood is relational with adulthood and defined in its difference from adulthood.

The low status of childhood in England is a matter for social concern. Why is it that adults routinely denigrate, suspect the morality of, disregard the efforts of an important social group? Why is it that adults so readily think of children as recipients of education, rather than as active participants in learning? Why are their contributions to establishing and promoting social relations not recognised or valued? We have to try to understand better why children have lowly status.

Central to the argument here is patriarchy – the unwillingness of those in power to relinquish it. After all, women are still fighting their own battles. Children are a long way behind.[12] As I suggested earlier, we can also point to the historical social contract between the generations, to the prevalent view – prevalent in England at least, that adults' main responsibility towards children is to protect them and provide for them; not to enable their social participation. And government policies and rhetoric are important in positioning children; New Labour has helped to solidify ideas by continuing to present children as suspect, needing to be tested; and as pre-citizens, needing control, guidance and supervision. Furthermore, as noted earlier, some adults confuse the physical, biological vulnerabilities of children with socially constructed vulnerabilities (Lansdown 1994). Thus stranger-danger and traffic danger are socially constructed dangers; they increase adult perceptions of children's vulnerability and the need for adult supervision. The consequent restriction of children to their homes also helps to give support to the view that children have no rightful presence in public places (unless with an adult). It's a vicious spiral.

One way to challenge children's low status is to give a good account of what they do contribute to the society they live in. This can be done, using the three sociologies of childhood. By collecting data with children we can empirically demonstrate their contributions. By describing how childhood is variously defined and understood (or constructed), we can bring critical thought to bear on the power of social constructions to mould our beliefs and actions. And by analysing childhood as relational – childhood as an integrated contributory social status – we can begin to shift ideas towards greater respect for children and for childhood itself.

Generation
Since childhood is relational with adulthood, the two social statuses inter-relate and changes in one will lead, in the end, to changes in the other. Thus, for example, if childhood gets defined as a vulnerable and incompetent stage in life, then adulthood will have to be defined as supervisory, controlling, protecting. I want here to focus on the concept of generation, which has potential for working towards understanding relational changes in childhood and adulthood, and these changes will include changes in educational thinking.

Generation as a concept is a big topic, which has been discussed extensively, following on from Mannheim's famous paper, first issued in 1928, on how cultural change takes place.[13] Here we can – briefly – discuss how cultural changes and institutional structures inter-relate.

On the cultural level, people born at differing times will have differing experiences and will form differing ideas about their identities and about their relations with other people. Childhood is changing in the industrialised world under the impacts of urbanisation, access to resources, consumerism and, perhaps most notably, the new technologies – television, computers, the internet (Buckingham 2000; Wyness 2000). Children's relations with each other, across the industrialised world, are being strengthened through access to technologies; some children see themselves as members of a Children's International (Hengst 2003); children are gathering strength, as a social group from their international, internet contacts. They are discussing their rights and wrongs across societies. Such changes in how childhood is lived, will impact on how children interact with adults, and how they interact with the institutions provided for them, such as schools.

So we have to consider these cultural changes in relation to the generational structures that define childhood in certain ways, through establishing and maintaining a range of institutions, laws, customs. In the case of the education system, we can see that schools are provided according to outdated principles, dating back to the start of state education. These principles have not shifted in response to changes in childhood. Children still get positioned as pupils, a generational position in relation to teachers. The generational position of childhood – in opposition to adulthood – gets established and reproduced through the institutions that organise it. Thus children can be seen as occupying a place in the generational order – just as, through feminist work, we began to understand women's and men's social positions as determined within the gender order.

So the idea of generation is active at both cultural and institutional levels, and changes at one level must, in the end, be reflected in differences at the other level. This dual, but interlinked, notion of generation is useful for trying to think about what to do about the education system in England. Cultural practices of childhood are changing, in response to a wide range of pressures, including technologies. Meanwhile the socio-structural position of children – as pupils in the structures of education – or more precisely schooling – is based on traditional ideas and is dysfunctional. It creates tensions between children and adults. There is a fault-line between how childhood is changing as a lived social culture, and how the education system understands children. And this fault-line provides the best hope for reform in the education system. A fascinating example of tension between older and newer ideas about childhood is provided in a recent DfES document: *Excellence and Enjoyment* (2003b), where there is constant slippage between use of the word 'pupils' and the word 'children', without any indication why one is preferred to the other in the immediate context. Old understandings confront newer ones.

An important topic within large-scale sociological work on childhood is to consider the social contract between generations. How far does the middle generation of those in power distribute resources to the previous generation – to the old, to themselves, and to the next generation, the young? It has been noted that in many welfare state societies the distribution of resources is prioritising the old (Thomson 1996); that in the UK those in power – the middle generation

– are taxing themselves lightly (Bradshaw 2002) and that children – who suffered badly in 18 years of Conservative government – are only slowly being lifted out of poverty.

It would seem that, in the UK, the generational contract between older and younger has not worked well in recent years. For those concerned with education, child poverty – including poor housing and run-down neighbourhoods – is a major barrier to educational success. The assault on child poverty is a prerequisite for children's engagement with formal education agendas (as Charles Dickens said). All that targeting of disadvantaged areas, through the EAZ scheme and more recently the Excellence in Cities scheme and Creative Partnerships, is very unlikely to make a significant difference to children's success in the formal attainments against which their educational achievement gets measured (*Guardian*, 2 June 2003).

How the sociology of childhood can help educational thinking

So we turn now to how the sociology of childhood and educational thinking can be inter-related. First a brief note on the well-known ills of the present education system in England.

What's wrong with the education system?
There is wide agreement that schools in England are not working well at present. Social class inequalities persist. Compulsion to attend is strongly emphasised while expulsions grow. Schools are counter-productive – they cause disaffection and children vote with their feet to avoid them. The implementation of the Education Reform Act 1988, with its testing and competition, has led to unhappiness amongst children and their teachers and has led schools to exclude children. Schools are adult-centred – they provide work for adults (Oldman 1994); and they serve the interests of the adult world. Even the notion of the child-centred school is discredited – since it is adults who define children's 'needs', abilities, readiness and so on (Walkerdine 1984; Woodhead 1990).

Indeed it can be argued that, like hooliganism (Pearson 1983), dysfunctional education has always been with us. Without again referring to my local hero Charles Dickens (e.g. *Hard Times*, 1854), we can certainly say that from the mid-nineteenth century to the present day, education has been in crisis in the UK (Richmond 1975). This crisis is linked to the social-class divisions on which the state education system was and is based (Walden 1996; Jeffs 2002); to unrealistic social reform expectations of the education service; to manipulation of the education system to suit the wishes of the governing elite (Sharp and Green 1975; Young and Whitty 1977). Writing in the mid-1970s, Kenneth Richmond (1975) deplored the then crisis in education and analysed distinctions between education and schooling, to the detriment of the providers of schooling. There is nothing new under the sun here.

How are children understood in the education system?

Put 20 or more children of roughly the same age in a little room, confine them to desks, make them wait in line, make them behave. It is as if a secret committee, now lost to history, had made a study of children and, having figured out what the greatest number were least disposed to do, declared that all of them should do it.

(quoted in Gardner 1993: 138)

But whilst crises in education may be always with us, it has been rare for educational thinkers to consider the central, determining importance of the traditional understandings of childhood that underpin the UK education system. And these constitute a major barrier to reform. Let us quickly emphasise some of the main ones.

Children are frequently described and understood as '*pupils*'; that is, as in subordinate social relations to their teachers. Children themselves tell us that they think they have no choice whatever during the school day. You just do what you are told (Mayall 2002: Chapter 7).

Children in the school system are also regarded as *incompetent*. Again, there is no need to dwell on this. Testing, marking, adult supervision, adult control over the subject-matter of learning, and the processes of learning are all indicators of denigration.

Children are understood as *immature*. This is shown in the discourses about attention-spans, poor ability to remain 'on task', distractability, poor memory, poor social skills; and it also links to suspicion about moral status.

Children are understood within the curriculum and the structures of the school day as *morally suspect*. Examples are many. Thus, children have (in general) no say in what they learn. A child's explanation for absence from school is unacceptable; only a parent's statement will suffice. Children have to ask permission to go to the lavatory. Teachers justify this – they must monitor children's trips to the lavatory, and limit them to the strictly necessary (in their view); otherwise all the children would be 'skiving off' (Mayall 1994: Chapters 4 and 5; 1996: Chapter 5). Yet in a Swedish school, I saw children quietly leaving the classroom for a few minutes and returning to get on with their work. No questions asked.

Definitions – or constructions – of children as *incompetent, immature, morally suspect pupils* have pervaded thinking in the education system. And these definitions constitute barriers to change. When proposals are made to free up children to act as learners, people will always reply, but children are not competent, not mature enough, not reliable enough to be freed up and to choose their learning programmes.

My point is that re-thinking childhood is a key central prerequisite for the long slow processes of improvement. We shall not make significant headway on re-thinking the education system towards something acceptable to children unless better ideas about childhood are both available and endorsed. These new approaches propose serious attention to children's own views as a precondition for successful schools. It is here that sociology of childhood can contribute, in complement to the children's rights movement.

Let us briefly revisit the three sociologies I outlined earlier.

- In the sociology of children, data collected with children and by children, is teaching us adults that children are knowledgeable, constructively critical social agents, competent, able to cope, resilient.

- The social construction of childhood leads us adults to question our assumptions, by recognising that they are tied into our social and political systems and goals.
- The structural sociology of childhood tells us that children are contributors to the social order. They do socially useful and indeed necessary things, including active engagement with learning, contributions to household and more general economies, and participation in building and promoting good social relations.

What ways forward are suggested?

So what do people suggest are ways forward for reforming the education system? Clearly, there is a long history of suggestions, some more utopian than others. But there is a good deal of common ground among the reformers. We should start by considering the views of those at the centre of the education system, those whose daily lives and futures are most affected by it – the children themselves.

Children's views on the schools they would like have been collected over at least the last three decades. And there is remarkable unanimity in the themes they present (Blishen 1969; Cullingford 1991; Mayall 1996; Triggs and Pollard 1998; Edwards 2002; Burke and Grosvenor 2003). Children draw on their private troubles – their current experience – in order to address public issues, and they come up with general proposals that chime in well with what adult reformers suggest. School students at both secondary and primary levels are in favour of education at school; they are not 'de-schoolers'. Above all, they ask for respect for themselves as persons and as learners. They want to learn, to choose what and when to learn, to have teachers who work as partners or enablers who help them learn. Many of them want to see a more open school, where students engage too with the outside world.

As Edward Blishen said in his introduction to his selection of student contributions to the 1967 *Guardian* newspaper competition, 'The School I'd Like', the key to a good school is to free up children to learn. Not just the very articulate, but young people of a range of abilities have in common the desire to be active learners:

children's longing to take upon themselves some of the burden of deciding what should be learnt, how it should be learnt: this desire to get closer to the raw matter of learning, not to be presented with predigested knowledge by teacher or textbook; above all to learn by talking, debating, with the teacher as senior confederate rather than the sole provider. They want excitement; they want a form of learning for which the word, for so many of them, is "research"; they want to discover how to be responsible for themselves and their own ideas. They want simply to discover.

(Blishen 1969: 10-11)

Here, in the same vein, is an excerpt from one of the winning submissions to the *Guardian* 2001 competition, 'The School I'd Like':

In my ideal school, the whole philosophy that dominates school now will be dropped.... There will be adults who like young people (and are) there to help us discover things.... Exams will not exist and neither will a one-size-fits-all curriculum. Pupils will decide what they want to learn and learn it.... Each project will be handed in not to be marked ... but to teach others about what the pupil has learned.... My ideal school will produce real people who respect and accommodate others. They will have been treated fairly and celebrated as individuals. Because they will have been encouraged instead of restrained, they will develop into creative, assertive people who will work together with their individual talents to rebuild the earth.

(from a *Guardian Education* report, 5 June 2001)

Adult reformers agree with the students. (Recent notables include: Gardner 1993; Meighan and Siraj-Blatchford 1997; Bentley 1998; Alderson 2003.) Some of the key points reformers make are:

- children are keen to learn
- children should be able to choose what to learn and when
- child–adult relations should be civil, respectful, creative and productive.

Of central importance is *civil* relations between the generations. Howard Gardner pinpoints this in his discussion of how to create environments in which children learn.

> Only if schools are concerned with civility, with fair treatment of all students from all groups, with feelings, interests, motivations and values, as well as with cognitive goals, can such an environment be constructed and sustained.
> (Gardner 1993: 243)

The implication of these points is that schools should be re-conceptualised as resource centres for children, where their resources for learning would include technologies as well as adults and other young people. Indeed it may be that the technological revolution will force through change. Children should be enabled to use local resources too, libraries, youth centres, drama clubs, sports grounds and centres, IT centres, nature reserves, museums. Some of this is happening and some of the people who staff these resources are keen to work with children. Children enjoy working with non-teachers and in settings other than school (Carnell and Meecham 2002; Mayall *et al.* 2003), on projects which are not subject to formal assessment and testing. Such settings promote opportunities for children to learn, to engage actively and to create their own interpretations of what they see, hear and do.

In sum, most reformers agree that learning should be freed up so that children are provided with a social environment that encourages them to maintain the interest in learning that they showed in their earliest years. The emphasis, as everyone notes, should be on learning and not on testing.

The central educational issue facing us in the twenty-first century is how to re-think the education service in such a way that it respects children as learners, respects children's rights, and promotes civil, respectful relations between children and those who help them learn.

Of key interest is ways in which the concept of generation can help us describe and study childhood's relations with adulthood (Mayall and Zeiher 2003). It seems ever more clear that the institutions set up 130 years ago to school our children are creaking under the impacts of cultural changes in how childhood is lived and in the social worlds children are growing up into. The generational order is changing as the cultural and the institutional clash – whether we like it or not. Children stress that they would like child–adult relations to be mutually respectful. Teachers' controlling behaviour should give way, they say, to friendly helpfulness, so that young people can learn in an ethos of respect.

What hope for change?

What hope is there in the UK social scene? Surely we are in a good position to re-think school. The system is not immutable; it is a mere 130 years old. We have good knowledge, derived from psychological and sociological studies as well as from participant observation, that children from the word go are keen learners, keen participators in social life. We can rely on them to want to learn. We can therefore work towards freeing up the curriculum, so that children take decisions about what to learn. Some of this is already happening in some schools. Much of the effort teachers have to put into controlling unwilling children could be channelled into helping children learn what they want to learn.

There are many examples of democratising initiatives in schools (Osler 2000). Schools have provided research arenas where people have been able to study the pros and cons of schooling; how well it works in practice. We have, as noted above, a lot of information – almost all pointing in the same direction – from young people themselves. We have vastly more educational resources than we had in 1870 – film, radio, TV, computers, IT networks and so on. We have long established traditions of creative activities in schools – drama, dance, visual arts, music – and these are coming back into fashion; we can build on those traditions. Local resources – libraries, sports centres, nature reserves and so on – have increased in numbers and range (though always under threat of cuts: should they be costed under education budgets, rather than 'leisure'?). All of these factors provide huge opportunities for re-thinking the education system in favour of children's learning and in favour of respect for children's wishes and interests.

Things are changing, and indeed quite fast over the last few years. Policy-makers are thinking about loosening up the compulsory school attendance agenda – shifting the balance between school and 'work'. At university level, there is an explosion of Childhood courses, which include attention to sociological accounts. Among these the Open University new first degree course (U212), with its first-rate publications, is likely to be very influential (Maybin and Woodhead 2003; Kehily and Swann 2003; Woodhead and Montgomery 2003; Montgomery, Burr and Woodhead 2003). The Institute of Education itself is putting a toe in the water (an MA in Childhood Studies is scheduled to start in the year 2003–4). Over the last dozen years masses of data have documented children's knowledge, experience and views.

The children's rights movement has made great progress in the UK, with rights officers in local authorities, and commissioners established in Scotland, Wales and Northern Ireland – but not yet in England (it will happen). Though the new English Minister for Children is responsible for all but education, yet within the education system itself children's participation in decision-making is being promoted, through conferences and publications and through practice. There is growing government recognition that children's participation in decision-making should be respected (DfES 2003a). There is considerable emphasis in government departments on fostering creativity in the education system – and fostering creativity demands, among other things, that students be conceptualised as active learners (e.g. Joubert 2001; QCA 2003).

We can note, too, that some pioneers are teaching children about their rights. A project in Nova Scotia (Covell and Howe 1999) has led to some English education authorities taking up the idea, and working with a child rights curriculum in primary and secondary schools. The UK government is of course duty-bound to inform children and adults of children's rights (UNCRC: Article 42); but has done little on this front. If we want to convince policy-makers that this is a good idea – one which may appeal to their concerns, we can point to research findings that when children learn about rights, their behaviour in school becomes more tolerant, more thoughtful, more democratic (Covell and Howe 1999).

At present the very rigour of government education initiatives starting in the early 1990s is itself producing a backlash in favour of change. Not just among children who vote with their feet. But also among teachers, who dislike having to do top-down prescribed teaching and having to control bored children; and who are concerned about unnecessary stress levels among children. Teachers experience on the ground the negative – prescriptive – sides of the literacy strategy and tell us that children learn best when they are actively engaged.[14] Currently there are signs of productive discussion between government and school teachers (DfES 2003b).

I should like everyone in the education system, at all levels, to think about models of childhood and about children's contributions to the social order. I should like a proper national debate on the quality of childhood experience as children live through their childhoods. This should include study of child experience in schools, and across the school and home (Edwards 2002). Schools themselves should make time for children to discuss childhood. Indeed any course of learning concerned with social relations must take up and problematise ideas about childhood and power issues in child–adult relations.

Universities have a key responsibility to promote discourse on childhood from a range of perspectives, sociological, psychological and anthropological. As I emphasised earlier, proper socio-political discourse on childhood is needed to promote basic conceptual thinking about how societies work, how all social groups contribute and interact. All teacher training should include such a range of approaches and considerations. Teachers themselves must be encouraged, not only to maintain an academic interest in developing themes and knowledge, not only to develop professionally, but perhaps most crucially to develop as persons – so that they may work in creative and productive ways with children (Prentice, Matthews and Taylor 2003).

Reforming the education system is like turning round a tanker. A huge effort has to be made to shift ideas as a firm basis for better policies. But as it begins to move the education system will steam ahead on new and exciting routes. And things are moving. Government's dawning recognition that children have participation rights, even in the education system, coupled with data collected with children, and the activities of rights organisations and commissioners for children in Wales, Scotland and Northern Ireland, are showing four main things. They are showing that children can be relied upon, trusted to participate sensibly. That children do have important, relevant points to make on social issues. That structures at all levels of government and planning are needed to enable effective participation to take place. And that without children's participation in planning and decision-making, services for children are unlikely to be successful.

If we think the education system should be changed – towards a system in which younger and older people act in alliance or partnership with each other, in which people learn, using technologies as well as teachers to help them, a system in which it is recognised that the school must respect children as learners if it is to play and important part in children's learning, then we adults must take seriously the view of the experts at the centre of the debate – the school students. And an important means towards change is to disseminate more adequate ideas about children and childhood than those currently in common circulation. It will take time, but things are moving.

Notes

1 In the 1970s the Thomas Coram Research Unit was sited in Brunswick Square. The Institute library was a fifteen-minute walk away – in Ridgmount Street. We worked on typewriters, manual and later electric. No personal computers – no email, no internet. Lots of hard memos and letters. Draft papers had to be typed and re-typed. The computers for data analysis were in the main Institute building, and occupied a whole room; data was punched onto cards and fed into a machine which located variables physically – using metal 'knitting needles'.

2 In the 1850s, Charles Dickens lived a few minutes from the Institute of Education, in a grand house just off Tavistock Square – where the British Medical Association building now is (Ackroyd 1991). (The remains of his house are in the grounds of the BMA building – but visible only to doctors.) Dickens is well known for his interest in education (Collins 1963), as demonstrated in his novels (e.g. *Nicholas Nickleby* and *Hard Times*). Perhaps less well known is that he was 'a frequent and fascinated visitor' to the first Froebel kindergarten in England – sited at 32 Tavistock Place, just around the corner from his house (Read, 2003; Collins 1963: 41). Dickens commissioned a paper on Froebel's ideas and on the kindergarten for his journal Household Words in July 1855 (Morley 1855).

Dickens walked to work at his office in Wellington Street (just off the Strand) through the grand new squares of the Bedford Estate (Tavistock, Gordon, Woburn and Russell) (Summerson 1962: Chapters 2, 3, 12), but he also frequently walked through the grimmest slums of London. He never ceased to argue, through papers (in his own journals: *Household Words* and *All the Year Round*) and speeches, that people needed decent housing, clean water and sanitation before they could be expected to benefit from schooling: 'Neither Religion nor Education will make any way, in this nineteenth century of Christianity, until a Christian government shall have discharged its first obligation, and secured to the people Homes, instead of polluted dens' (*Household Words*, 7 October 1854, reprinted as Paper 29 'To Working Men', in Slater 1998; quoted and discussed in Slater 1999: 140–2).

3 I have discussed feminist neglect of the sociology of childhood elsewhere (Mayall 2002: especially Chapter 9). Just as the sociology of childhood can learn from feminism, so feminism can learn from it. And the two political enterprises can and should work together, for better conceptual understanding.

4 The same phenomenon can be seen in feminist work. In the 1970s young women studied young women and issues of immediate importance to them – sexual relations, child-care, housework. Only as they got older themselves did they begin to study older women and associated issues.

5 See also for discussion of the relative contributions of biology and social experience to child development, Greene 1999.

6 A useful recent discussion of socialisation and development theories is given by Maybin and Woodhead (2003: Chapter 1).

7 For discussion of Beck, in relation to recent data, notably from the ESRC Children 5–16 Programme, see also Prout 2000.

8 The Children's Society was founded in 1881 as the Church of England Central Home for Waifs and Strays. In 1946 its title changed to the Church of England Children's Society and in 1982 it adopted the informal title of 'The Children's Society'.

9 The four Institute of Education ESRC-funded projects on the Children 5–16 Programme were directed by Alderson, Candappa, Joshi and Mayall.

10 RoutledgeFalmer is issuing a series of books under the general title The Future of Childhood, each of which takes a particular theme and has papers arising from the Children 5–16 Programme and others drawing on international research studies (so far: Alanen and Mayall 2001; Mizen, Pole and Bolton 2001; Jensen and McKee 2002; Edwards 2002; Christensen and O'Brien 2003).

11 A number of UK studies have demonstrated, through a range of methods, that children's work is an important aspect of their daily lives, whether paid or unpaid, in or out of the home (Morrow 1994, 1996; Mizen, Pole and Bolton 2001; Mayall 2002: Chapter 5).

12 Elsewhere I have suggested that we would do well to try to put feminist and childhood studies together, in order to provide a better understanding of children's relations with women, through the life-course; and in order to make common cause against patriarchy (Alanen 1992; Mayall 2002: Chapter 9).

13 Mannheim 1952 [1928]; Pilcher 1994; Alanen 2001; Edmunds and Turner 2002; Mayall 2002: Chapters 3 and 9; Mayall and Zeiher 2003.

14 Data on these topics are being collected in a Social Science Research Unit research project studying the National Theatre's drama work in primary schools (Mayall, Turner, Wiggins, Hood and Dickinson 2003).

References

Ackroyd, P. (1991) Dickens. London: Minerva paperbacks.
Alanen, L. (1992) *Modern Childhood? Exploring the 'child question' in sociology*. Research Report 50. Finland: University of Jyväskylä.
—— (2001) 'Explorations in generational analysis'. In L. Alanen and B. Mayall (eds), *Conceptualizing Child-adult Relations*. London: RoutledgeFalmer.
Alanen, L. and Mayall, B. (eds) (2001) *Conceptualizing Child-adult Relations*. London: RoutledgeFalmer.
Alderson, P. (2003) *Institutional Rites and Rights: A century of childhood*. London: Institute of Education
Aldridge, J. and Becker, S. (2002) 'Children who care: rights and wrongs in debate and policy on young carers'. In B. Franklin (ed.), *The New Handbook of Children's Rights: Comparative policy and practice*. London: Routledge.

Beck, U. (1992) *Risk Society: Towards a new modernity.* London: Sage.
Bentley, T. (1998) *Learning Beyond the Classroom: Education for a changing world.* London: RoutledgeFalmer.
Bilton, T, Bennett, K., Jones, P., Lawson, T., Skinner, D., Stanworth, M. and Webster, A. (2002) *Introductory Sociology*, 4th edition. London: Palgrave Macmillan.
Blishen, E. (1969) *The School that I'd Like.* Harmondsworth: Penguin.
Bradshaw, J. (2002) 'Child poverty and child outcomes', *Children and Society*, 16, 2: 131–40.
Browne, K. (1998) *An Introduction to Sociology*, 2nd edition. Cambridge: Polity Press.
Bruce, M. (1979) *The Coming of the Welfare State.* London: Batsford.
Buckingham, D. (2000) *After the Death of Childhood: Growing up in the age of electronic media.* Cambridge: Polity Press.
Burke, C. and Grosvenor, I. (2003) *The School I'd Like: Children and young people's reflections on an education for the 21st Century.* London: RoutledgeFalmer.
Carnell, E. and Meecham, P. (2002) *Visual paths to literacy. A final report on a three-year research project.* London: Institute of Education, Department of Art, Design and Museology.
Christensen, P. and James, A. (eds) (2000) *Research with Children: Perspectives and practices.* London: RoutledgeFalmer.
Christensen, P. and O'Brien, M. (eds) (2003) *Children in the City: Home, neighbourhood and community.* London: RoutledgeFalmer.
Cole, M. (1996) *Cultural Psychology.* Cambridge, MA: Harvard University Press.
Collins, P. (1963) *Dickens and Education.* London: Macmillan.
Covell, K. and Howe, B. (1999) 'The impact of children's rights education: A Canadian study', *International Journal of Children's Rights*, 7: 171–83.
Cullingford, C. (1991) *The Inner World of the School.* London: Cassell.
Cunningham, H. (1991) *The Children of the Poor: Representations of childhood since the seventeenth century.* Oxford: Blackwell.
—— (2003) 'Children's changing lives from 1800 to 2000'. In J. Maybin and M. Woodhead (eds), *Childhoods in Context.* London: John Wiley in association with The Open University.

Damon, W. (1990) *The Moral Child: Nurturing children's natural moral growth.* New York: The Free Press.

DfES (Department for Education and Skills) (2003a) 'Working together: Giving children and young people a say'. Participation Guidance, 17.7.2003. Online. Available HTTP: <www.dfes.gov.uk/consultations2/18/docs/ParticipationGuidanceforConsultation.doc> (accessed 18 August 2003).

——(2003b) *Excellence and Enjoyment: A strategy for primary schools.* London: DfES.

Dunn, J. (1988) *The Beginnings of Social Understanding.* Oxford: Blackwell.

Durkheim, E. (1961) *Moral Education: A study in the theory and application of the sociology of education.* New York: Free Press of Glencoe (first published 1912).

Edmunds, J. and Turner, B.S. (2002) *Generations, Culture and Society.* Buckingham: Open University Press.

Edwards, R. (ed.) (2002) *Children, Home and School: Regulation, autonomy or connection?* London: RoutledgeFalmer.

Freeman, M. (2000) 'The future of children's rights', *Children and Society*, 14, 4: 277–93.

Fulcher, J and Scott, J. (1999) *Sociology.* Oxford: Oxford University Press.

Gardner, H. (1993) *The Unschooled Mind.* London: Fontana Press.

Gavron, K. (1997) 'Migrants to citizens: Changing orientations among Bangladeshis of Tower Hamlets'. Unpublished PhD thesis. London University.

Gibbs, S., Mann, G. and Mathers, N. (2002) *Child-to-Child: A practical guide: Empowering children as active citizens.* London: Upstream.

Giddens, A. (2001) *Sociology*, 4th edition. Cambridge: Polity Press.

Gordon, T., Holland, J. and Lahlema, E. (2000) *Making Spaces: Citizenship and difference in schools.* London: Macmillan.

Greater London Authority (2003) *Towards a Child-friendly London: The Mayor's draft children and young people's strategy.* London: Greater London Authority.

Greene, S. (1999) 'Child development: old themes, new directions'. In M. Woodhead, D. Faulkner and K. Littleton (eds), *Making Sense of Social Development.* London and New York: Routledge in association with The Open University.

Haralambos, M., Holborn, M. and Heald, R. (2000) *Sociology: Themes and perspectives*, 5th edition. London: HarperCollins.

Hart, R. (1997) *Children's Participation*. London: Earthscan Publications.

Hendrick, H. (1990) 'Constructions and reconstructions of British childhood: An interpretative survey, 1800 to the present'. In A. James and A. Prout (eds), *Constructing and Reconstructing Childhood: Contemporary issues in the sociological study of childhood*. London: Falmer.

Hendrick, H. (1994) *Child Welfare, England 1872–1989*. London: Routledge.

—— (2003) *Child Welfare: Historical dimensions, contemporary debate*. Bristol: Policy Press.

Hengst, H. (2003) 'The role of media and commercial culture in children's experiencing of collective identities'. In B. Mayall and H. Zeiher (eds), *Childhood in Generational Perspective*. London: Institute of Education.

Holman, B. (2001) *Champions for Children: the lives of modern child care pioneers*. Bristol: Policy Press.

Hurt, J.S. (1979) *Elementary Schooling and the Working Classes 1860–1918*. London: Routledge and Kegan Paul.

James, A. and Jenks, C (1996) 'Public perceptions of childhood criminality', *British Journal of Sociology*, 47, 2: 315–31.

Jeffs, T. (2002) 'Schooling, education and children's rights'. In B. Franklin (ed.), *The New Handbook of Children's Rights: Comparative policy and practice*. London: Routledge.

Jenks, C. (1996) *Childhood*. London: Fontana.

Jensen, A.-M. and McKee, L. (eds) (2002) *Children and the Changing Family: Between transformation and negotiation*. London: RoutledgeFalmer.

Johnson, V., Hill, J. and Ivan-Smith, E. (1995) *Listening to Smaller Voices: Children in an environment of change*. London: Action Aid.

Johnson, V., Ivan-Smith, E., Gordon, G., Pridmore, P. and Scott, P. (1998) *Stepping Forward: Children and young people's participation in the development process*. London: Intermediate Technology Publications.

Joubert, M. (2001) 'The art of creative teaching: NACCCE and beyond'. In A. Craft, B. Jeffrey and M. Leibling (eds), *Creativity in Education*. London: Continuum.

Kagitcibasi, C. (1996) *Family and Human Development: A view from the other side.* Hove: Lawrence Erlbaum.

Kehily, M.J. and Swann, J. (eds) (2003) *Children's Cultural Worlds.* Chichester: John Wiley in association with the Open University.

Key, E. (1909) *The Century of the Child.* New York: G.P. Putnam (first published in Sweden 1900).

La Fontaine, J.S. (1998) 'Are children people?'. In J.S. La Fontaine and H. Rydstrøm (eds), *The Invisibility of Children. Papers presented at an international conference on anthropology and children, May 1997.* Linköping University, Sweden: Department of Child Studies.

Lansdown, G. (1994) 'Children's rights'. In B. Mayall (ed.) *Children's Childhoods: Observed and experienced.* London: Falmer.

Mackinnon, D. (2003) 'Children and work'. In J. Maybin and M. Woodhead (eds), *Childhoods in Context.* Chichester: John Wiley in association with The Open University.

Mannheim, K. (1952) 'The problem of generations'. In K. Mannheim (ed.) *Essays in the Sociology of Knowledge.* London: Routledge and Kegan Paul (first published 1928).

Mayall, B. (1994) *Negotiating Health: Children at home and primary school.* London: Cassell.

—— (1996) *Children, Health and the Social Order.* Buckingham: Open University Press.

—— (1998) 'Towards a sociology of child health'. *Sociology of Health and Illness*, 20, 3: 269–88.

—— (2002) *Towards a Sociology for Childhood: Thinking from children's lives.* Buckingham: Open University Press.

Mayall, B. and Zeiher, H. (eds) (2003) *Childhood in Generational Perspective.* London: Institute of Education.

Mayall, B., Turner, H., Wiggins, M., Hood S. and Dickinson, R. (2003) 'Evaluation of the National Theatre Education Department's drama work in primary schools'. Interim report. January. London: Social Science Research Unit, Institute of Education.

Maybin, J. and Woodhead, M. (2003) 'Socializing children'. In J. Maybin and M.

Woodhead (eds), *Childhoods in Context*. Chichester: John Wiley in association with the Open University.

Meighan, R. and Siraj-Blatchford, I. (1997) *A Sociology of Educating*, 3rd edition. London: Cassell.

Mizen, P., Bolton, A. and Pole, C. (1999) 'School age workers in Britain: The paid employment of children in Britain'. *Work, Employment and Society*, 13, 3: 423–38.

Mizen, P., Pole, C. and Bolton, A. (eds) (2001) *Hidden Hands: International perspectives on children's work and labour*. London: RoutledgeFalmer.

Montgomery, H., Burr, R. and Woodhead, M. (eds) (2003) *Changing Childhoods: Local and global*. Chichester: John Wiley in association with the Open University.

Morley, H. (1855) 'Infant gardens', *Household Words*, no. 278 (21 July).

Morrow, V. (1994) 'Responsible children: Aspects of children's work and employment outside school in contemporary UK'. In B. Mayall (ed.), *Children's Childhoods: Observed and experienced*. London: Falmer.

—— (1996) 'Rethinking childhood dependence: Children's contributions to the domestic economy'. *Sociological Review*, 44, 1: 58–76.

Oakley, A. (1994), 'Women and children first and last: Parallels and differences between children's and women's studies'. In B. Mayall (ed.), *Children's Childhoods: Observed and experienced*. London: Falmer.

Office of the Children's Rights Commissioner for London (2003) *A Legacy and a Challenge for London: A three-year demonstration project – final report*. London: OCRCL.

Oldman, D. (1994) 'Childhood as a mode of production'. In B. Mayall (ed.), *Children's Childhoods: Observed and experienced*. London: Falmer.

Osler, A. (ed.) (2000) *Citizenship and Democracy in Schools: Diversity, identity, equality*. Stoke-on-Trent: Trentham Books.

Pearson, G. (1983) *Hooligan: A history of respectable fears*. Basingstoke: Macmillan.

Pilcher, J. (1994) ' Mannheim's sociology of generations: An undervalued legacy', *British Journal of Sociology*, 45, 3: 481–95.

Prentice, R., Matthews, J. and Taylor H. (2003) 'Creative Development: Creativity, children's drawing, art design and music education'. In J. Riley (ed.), *Learning in the Early Years: A guide for teachers of 3–7.* London: Paul Chapman.

Pringle, K. (1998) *Children and Social Welfare in Europe.* Buckingham: Open University Press.

Prout, A. (1999) *The Body, Childhood and Society.* London: Macmillan.

—— (2000) 'Children's participation: Control and self-realisation in British late modernity'. Children and Society, 14, 4: 304–15.

Prout, A. and James, A. (1990) 'A new paradigm for the sociology of childhood? Provenance, promise and problems'. In A. James and A. Prout (eds), *Constructing and Reconstructing Childhood: Contemporary issues in the sociological study of childhood.* London: Falmer.

QCA (2003) 'Creativity: Find it, promote it'. Online. Available HTTP: <www.ncaction.org.uk/creativity> (accessed 18 August 2003).

Qvortrup, J. (1985) 'Placing children in the division of labour'. In R. Close and R. Collins (eds), *Family and Economy in Modern Society.* London: Macmillan.

Read, J. (2003) Froebelian women: networking to promote professional status and educational change in the nineteenth century. *History of Education*, 32, 1: 17–34.

Reid, I. (1978) Sociological Perspectives on School and Education. London: Open Books.

Richmond, W.K. (1975) *Education and Schooling.* London: Methuen.

Rogoff, B. (1990) *Apprenticeship in Thinking: Cognitive development in social context.* New York: Oxford University Press.

Rose, N. (1985) *The Psychological Complex: Psychology, politics and society in England 1869–1939.* London: Routledge and Kegan Paul.

Sharp, R. and Green, A. (1975) *Education and Social Control.* London: Routledge and Kegan Paul.

Shilling, C. (1993) *The Body and Social Theory.* London: Sage.

Slater, M. (1998) *Dickens' Journalism.* Vol. 3. London: J.M. Dent.

—— (1999) *An Intelligent Person's Guide to Dickens.* London: Gerald Duckworth.

Stacey, M. (1981) 'The division of labour revisited, or overcoming the two Adams'. In P. Abrams, R. Deem, J. Finch and P. Roch (eds), *Practice and Progress in British Sociology 1950–1980.* London: Allen and Unwin.

Stafseng, O. (1993) 'A sociology of childhood and youth – the need of both?'. In J. Qvortrup (ed.), *Childhood as a Social Phenomenon: Lessons from an international project*. Eurosocial Report 47/1993. Vienna: European Centre.

Summerson, J. (1962) *Georgian London*. Harmondsworth: Penguin Books.

Therborn, G. (1993) 'Children's rights since the constitution of modern childhood: A comparative study of western nations'. In J. Qvortrup (ed.), *Childhood as a Social Phenomenon: Lessons from an international project*. Eurosocial Report 47/1993. Vienna: European Centre.

—— (1996), 'Child politics: Dimensions and perspectives'. *Childhood*, 3, 1: 29–44.

Thomson, D. (1996) 'Justice between generations and the plight of children'. In H. Wintersberger (ed.), *Children on the Way from Marginality towards Citizenship. Childhood Policies: Conceptual and Practical Issues*. Eurosocial Report 61/1996. Vienna: European Centre.

Triggs, P. and Pollard, A. (1998) 'Pupil experience and a curriculum for life-long learning'. In C. Richards and P.H. Taylor (eds), *How Shall We School our Children? Primary education and its future*. London: Falmer.

Turner, B.S. (1992) *Regulating Bodies: Essays in medical sociology*. London: Routledge.

Walden, G. (1996) *We Should Know Better: Bridging the education crisis*. London: Fourth Estate.

Walkerdine, V. (1984) 'Developmental psychology and the child-centred pedagogy: The insertion of Piaget into early education'. In J. Henriques, W. Hollway, C. Urwin, C. Venn and V. Walkerdine, *Changing the Subject*. London: Methuen.

Woodhead, M. (1990) 'Psychology and the cultural construction of children's needs'. In A. James and A. Prout (eds), *Constructing and Reconstructing Childhood: Contemporary issues in the sociological study of childhood*. London: Falmer.

Woodhead, M. and Montgomery, H. (eds) (2003) *Understanding Childhood: An interdisciplinary approach*. Chichester: John Wiley in association with the Open University.

Wyness, M. (2000) *Contesting Childhood*. London: Falmer.

Young, B. and Durston, S. (1987) *Primary Health Education*. London: Longman.

Young, M. and Whitty, G. (1977) *Society, State and Schooling*. Lewes: Falmer.

Zeiher, H. (2003) 'Intergenerational relations and social change in childhood: Examples from West Germany'. In B. Mayall and H. Zeiher (eds), *Childhood in Generation Perspective*. London: Institute of Education.

Zelizer, V. (1985) *Pricing the Priceless Child: The changing social value of children*. New York: Basic Books.